D0822715

Put Beginning Readers on the Right Track
ALL ABOARD READING™

The All Aboard Reading series is especially designed for beginning readers. Written by noted authors and illustrated in full color, these are books that children really want to read—books to excite their imagination, expand their interests, make them laugh, and support their feelings. With fiction and nonfiction stories that are high interest and curriculum-related, All Aboard Reading books offer something for every young reader. And with four different reading levels, the All Aboard Reading series lets you choose which books are most appropriate for your children and their growing abilities.

Picture Readers
Picture Readers have super-simple texts, with many nouns appearing as rebus pictures. At the end of each book are 24 flash cards—on one side is a rebus picture; on the other side is the written-out word.

Station Stop 1
Station Stop 1 books are best for children who have just begun to read. Simple words and big type make these early reading experiences more comfortable. Picture clues help children to figure out the words on the page. Lots of repetition throughout the text helps children to predict the next word or phrase—an essential step in developing word recognition.

Station Stop 2
Station Stop 2 books are written specifically for children who are reading with help. Short sentences make it easier for early readers to understand what they are reading. Simple plots and simple dialogue help children with reading comprehension.

Station Stop 3
Station Stop 3 books are perfect for children who are reading alone. With longer text and harder words, these books appeal to children who have mastered basic reading skills. More complex stories captivate children who are ready for more challenging books.

In addition to All Aboard Reading books, look for All Aboard Math Readers™ (fiction stories that teach math concepts children are learning in school); All Aboard Science Readers™ (nonfiction books that explore the most fascinating science topics in age-appropriate language); and All Aboard Poetry Readers™ (funny, rhyming poems for readers of all levels).

All Aboard for happy reading!

For Mom and Dad

(the *original* Tickle Monster!)—D.S.

For Dad, who always told a good story

—A.S.

The scanning, uploading, and distribution of this book via the Internet or via any other means without the permission of the publisher is illegal and punishable by law. Please purchase only electronic editions and do not participate in or encourage electronic piracy of copyrighted materials. Your support of the author's rights is appreciated.

Text copyright © 2004 by David Steinberg. Illustrations copyright © 2004 by Adrian Sinnot. All rights reserved. Published by Grosset & Dunlap, a division of Penguin Young Readers Group, 345 Hudson Street, New York, New York 10014. GROSSET & DUNLAP and ALL ABOARD POETRY READER are trademarks of Penguin Group (USA) Inc. Printed in the U.S.A.

Library of Congress Cataloging-in-Publication Data

Steinberg, David, 1962–
  Grasshopper pie and other poems / by David Steinberg ; illustrated by Adrian Sinnott.
     p. cm. — (All aboard poetry reader. Station stop 2)
  Summary: Five poems celebrate the making of a very special pie, an upside-down boy, a sneezing elephant, an encounter with a monster, and an alien who lands in a bowl of chicken soup.
   ISBN 0-448-43491-1 — ISBN 0-448-43347-8 (pbk.)
   1. Children's poetry, American. [1. Humorous poetry. 2. American poetry.] I. Sinnott, Adrian C., ill II. Title. III. Series.
  PS3619.T47618 G73 2004
  811'.6—dc22
                    2003014177

ISBN 0-448-43347-8 (pbk)   A B C D E F G H I J

ISBN 0-448-43491-1 (GB)   A B C D E F G H I J

Grasshopper Pie
and Other Poems

by David Steinberg

illustrated by Adrian Sinnott

Grosset & Dunlap • New York

Table of Contents

Grasshopper Pie

I'm Grandma's favorite helper.

You should have seen her eyes

When I brought six grasshoppers

To make grasshopper pies!

I knew she'd want a closer look—

I opened up the lid.

I think those 'hoppers got confused—

They all hopped out and hid!

One jumped in the pantry

And one jumped in the sink.

One jumped into Grandma's cup

And tried to take a drink.

One went for the
chocolate cake.

Another found the bread.

Another one liked
Grandma—

He jumped right on
her head!

Grandma sure loves grasshoppers

As I could plainly tell.

Why, she got so excited,

She gasped and nearly fell.

I climbed across the counters

And scaled the pantry wall.

I hopped and jumped around the room

Till I had caught them all.

And that's when Grandma told me—

And my Grandma never lies—

There really are no grasshoppers

Inside grasshopper pies!

I stood in shock and disbelief.

(The grasshoppers just sighed.)

Then Grandma told my grasshoppers

To go and play outside.

Then she took a piecrust,

Scooped in some mint ice cream,

And made the best grasshopper pie—

With <u>me</u> on Grandma's team!

I'm Grandma's favorite helper—

Next day, I came to bake.

I brought a bag of marbles

To make a marble cake!

The Legend of Billy Ray Brown

This is the story of Billy Ray Brown

Who, legend is told, was born upside-down.

Instead of a head where one usually goes,

The doctor was greeted by ten wiggling toes.

When Billy Ray Brown learned to sit in a chair,

He sat on his nose with his legs in the air.

And he ate just like that from the day he could eat.

He became quite a pro using spoons with his feet.

When he learned how to stand,

Billy stood on his head.

And he slept with his toes on the pillow instead.

At school, all the children would watch him with awe

Whenever young Billy would sit down to draw.

He'd wiggle his rear, holding crayons with his knees,

Drawing upside-down pictures of houses and trees.

Soon Billy was winning the school talent
shows

By plucking the banjo with only his toes.

When he played Little League, his pa sat in the stands,

Shouting, "Run, Billy Ray! That's using your hands!"

That boy was the pride of his father and mother,

But Fan Number One was his own little brother.

Wherever he'd go, Jimmy Joe would go, too,

And whatever he did, Jimmy Joe tried to do.

But one night, he heard Jimmy crying in bed.

"Why am I so different?" his young brother said.

You see, little Jimmy Joe walked with his feet,

And when he sat down, put his tush on the seat!

"That's what makes you YOU!" said Billy Ray Brown,

But his upside-up brother was still feeling down.

Billy flipped Jimmy over. "See, in every frown,

Is a bright shining smile just turned upside-down!"

And to this very day, that's the cure for a frown:

Just go stand on your head . . .

like Billy Ray Brown!

Louise's Sneezes

You'll never meet an elephant

As lovely as Louise.

She wears a very lovely trunk

That curls down to her knees.

And she's really quite polite.

She says, "Thank you."

She says, "Please."

BUT . . .

She never covers up her trunk

When she has to sneeze!

Her mama says, "Remember,"

But Louise will just forget,

So if her trunk begins to twitch,

Beware—you might get wet.

Her friends will all skedaddle

When they hear a sniffle brewing;

They hold their ears and scrunch their eyes

Each time she starts a-chooing!

A-CHOO!

Her sneezes echo

Far across the grassy plains.

A-CHOO!

They twirl zebras' tails

And tangle lions' manes.

One day, she met a chimpanzee

Out selling some bananas—

A-CHOO!

It rained banana peels

For days through the savannas!

At recess time, while jumping rope,

She couldn't squelch a sneeze—

A-CHOO!

Her friends all landed

In some weeping wattle

trees!

And though she said, "Excuse me,"

As politely as she could,

I'm told Louise must now stay late

Each day at school for good.

So whenever your nose tickles,

Please remember what to do—

Learn a lesson from Louise

And cover up when you a-choo!

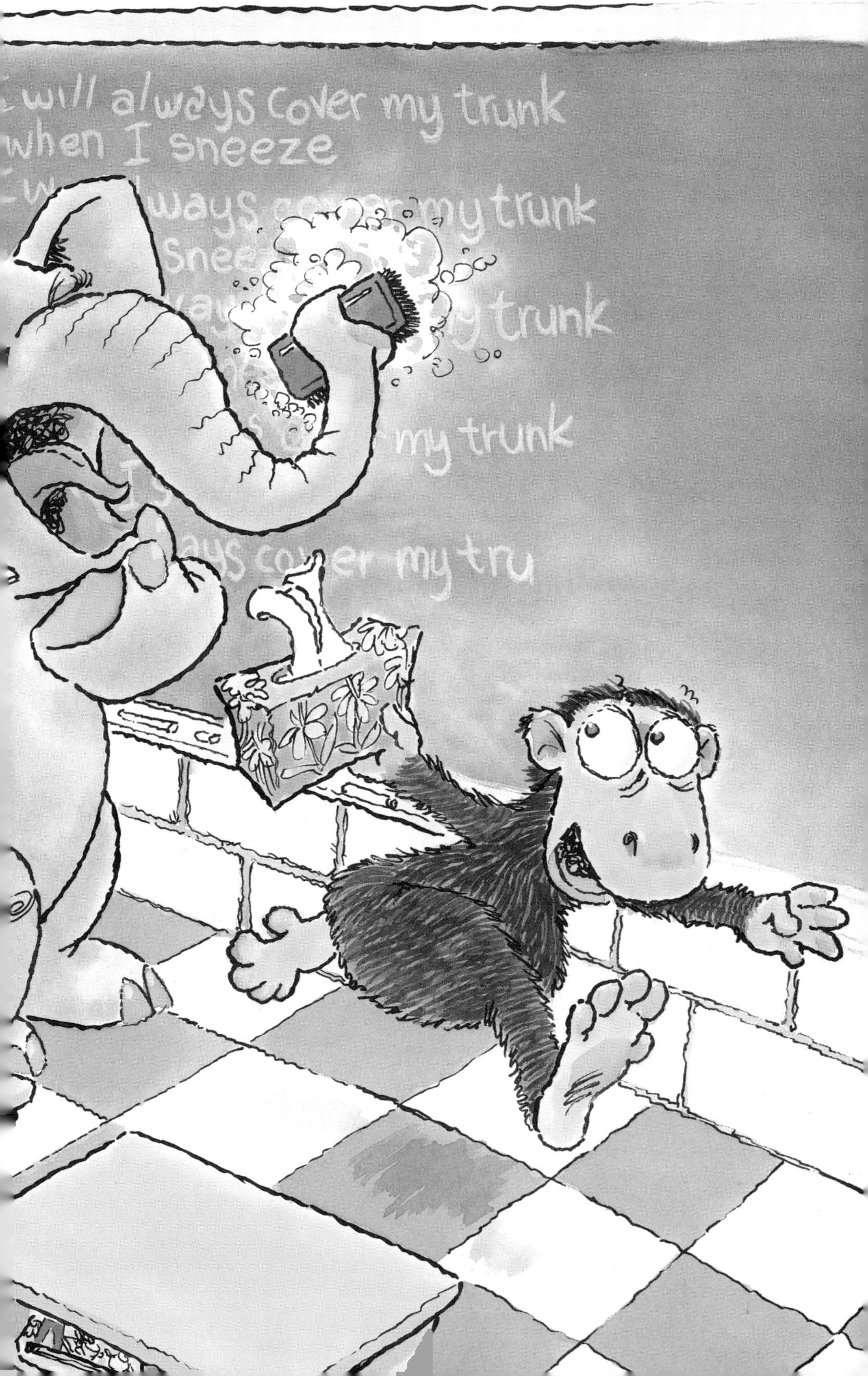
will always cover my trunk
when I sneeze

The Tickle Monster

One day, my boring dad

Was snoring in his chair,

But when I turned around,

I found the Tickle Monster there!

He chased me 'round the table,

Then I raced across the floor.

But the Tickle Monster caught me

Just before I reached the door.

With a Tickle to the belly

And a Tickle to the neck

And a Tickle to the toes,

I became a Tickle Wreck!

I wiggled and I giggled,

But I couldn't jiggle free.

When I tried to call for help,

It came out "Hee hee hee!"

Then the Tickle Monster finished

With a final Tickle Laugh;

I was tangled like a pretzel

And folded up in half!

When I sat back up again,

The Monster wasn't there;

Just my daddy with his feet up,

Snoozing in his chair.

An Alien in My Soup

An alien landed in my chicken soup!

While slurping my noodles, I heard a bloop.

He was goopy and green and not too tall.

His spaceship looked like a matzo ball.

I watched him as he bobbled past,

Frightening the rice with his laser blast.

I heard some squash squeak, "Rescue <u>meeeee</u>!"

"Someone call the cops!" cried the celery.

"Surrender," said the alien, "to my delicious crime:

I'm taking your planet, one bowl at a time!"

He sneered up at me, "No ifs, ands, or buts.

Your world will be mine, from soup to nuts!"

I realized right then: It was all up to me.

I had to rescue our whole galaxy!

So I opened my mouth, gulped that big matzo ball,

And ate up my soup, evil spaceman and all!